Handmade

Embroidered Purses

using free machine embroidery

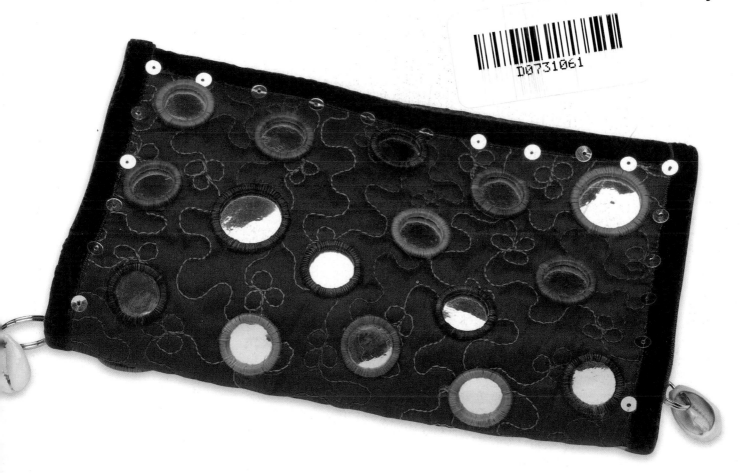

For Barry, Tiffany and Ashley, my
wonderful family, for their support,
help and encouragement.

Handmade
Embroidered
Purses *Jenny Rolfe*

using free machine embroidery

SEARCH PRESS

First published in Great Britain 2007

Search Press Limited
Wellwood, North Farm Road,
Tunbridge Wells, Kent TN2 3DR

Text copyright © Jenny Rolfe 2007

Photographs by Roddy Paine Photographic Studios
Photographs and design copyright
© Search Press Ltd 2007

ISBN-10: 1-84448-174-3
ISBN-13: 978-1-84448-174-3

Acknowledgements

*I would like to thank Arterial of Cosby for
supplying me with a number of threads, beads
and fabrics for this book and also
craftynotions.com for supplying me with
bondable fibres and threads among other things.*

*For helping me to proofread my projects, I would
like to thank my friend, Carole Wood.*

*Finally thank you to everyone at Search Press,
particularly Sophie, my editor, Juan for his
artistic talents, Roz Dace for first noticing my
work and Roddy for the wonderful photography.*

Publisher's note
All the step-by-step photographs in this book
feature the author, Jenny Rolfe, demonstrating
the making of embroidered purses. No models
have been used.

Front cover: The main purse shown is based on the
Velvet Purse project (see page 70). It has tiny buttons
sewn on and is finished with a handmade brooch (see
page 28).

Page 1: A purse based on the Indian Purse project (see
page 30). This one is made in dupion silk with hand-
covered shisha glass.

Page 3: This purse is based on the Box Purse project on
page 62 and has machine-embroidered appliqué circles
with buttons sewn on.

Contents

Introduction

Ever since I was a child I have liked containers, whether they were boxes, bags or purses. I think this is a natural instinct in girls and women, to gather, collect, organise and keep safe special items.

My grandparents lived by the sea and they had a beach hut. I used to love nothing more than collecting shells, interesting stones and general flotsam and jetsam from the beach and storing them away in the beach hut. I would use old shoe boxes, any tin that had a lid or even empty matchboxes if the shells were small enough.

When I learned to sew as a child, special fabrics such as silk and velvet were precious, so any bits left over from my mother's and grandmother's dressmaking were carefully stored away in my own sewing box. I remember having a small purse that my mother had embroidered, in which I kept special buttons. I still have some of the buttons, but alas the embroidered purse is long gone.

I suppose it was only a matter of time before I started making my own bags and purses, and there is a great satisfaction in making a purse that reflects the uniqueness and individuality of the creator.

There are times when all you need is a purse rather than a larger bag. It just needs to hold today's essentials such as a credit card, phone and lipstick. As purses need to be secure, I have used zips and magnetic clasps to keep the contents safe.

Some of the purses in this book are made using free machine embroidery. Do not worry if you have not done this before, as I explain it in detail in the Techniques section, and I suggest some of the patterns you can create. It can be done using a basic sewing machine.

The purses can be fun, they can be sensible, they can be sophisticated and they can reflect your own personality – this can be done by simply adding a bow or a buckle. Most of all they must be enjoyed.

Materials
Fabric

For these purses I have used easily obtainable fabrics such as cottons, silks and velvet, and I have chosen them mostly in plain colours rather than patterned. This is because I want the embroidery and embellishment to stand out. These fabrics can be found in any haberdashery shop. Fabrics that you have dyed yourself are also very useful.

Threads

Machine embroidery threads You can use more or less any thread on the sewing machine, but I particularly like the variegated ones. If I am sewing on cotton, I usually use the cotton threads and if I am sewing on silk I use rayon threads, but there are no hard and fast rules. The rayon threads add a beautiful sheen to your sewing.

Metallic threads There are many metallic threads on the market, some easier to use than others. To avoid the thread snapping, always use an appropriate machine needle. Either use a 'top stitch' needle or a 'metallic' needle.

Hand embroidery threads I use these to enhance and embellish my work by couching and using simple embroidery stitches. Threads such as perlé, fine ribbons, cotton à broder and crochet threads are useful, and so are gimp and fine cords.

Invisible thread I find invisible thread invaluable. It comes in light and dark shades. I use it mostly for couching down thicker threads and ribbons and for sewing sequins or beads on to a background. It is not really suitable for hand sewing.

Sewing machine

A basic sewing machine, not necessarily the specialist machine shown below, is all you need to make the purses in this book. As long as you can either lower the feed dogs or cover the plate, you can free machine. Your machine should be kept clean and oiled (if appropriate) all the time. Clean the bobbin area regularly as it very quickly becomes clogged.

Machine feet

Your machine will come with a number of feet. For the purposes of this book you will need a standard foot for straight stitching and a darning foot for free machining; an appliqué foot which is open at the front; a zipper foot and a walking foot, which helps to feed the fabric through evenly, making difficult fabrics much easier to sew.

Shown here from left to right are, back row: a walking foot, an appliqué foot and a standard foot; front row: a darning foot with an open front, a basic darning foot and a zipper foot.

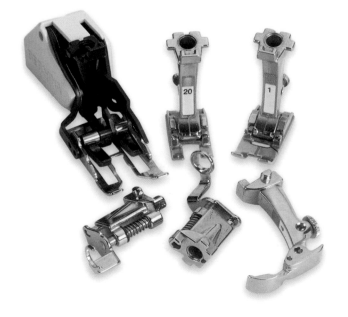

Basic sewing equipment

Scissors You will need a large pair of scissors for cutting fabric and a small, sharp-pointed pair for cutting threads. Curved scissors are useful but not essential and are used for snipping threads in awkward places.

Pins I like to use the flower-headed or glass-headed variety – they are very long and sharp, and if I drop one on the floor, I can find it easily (very useful when you have animals or small children in the house).

Machine needles I have a selection of needles, but I mostly like to use 'top stitch' needles. They are good for most machining purposes including free machining as they have long eyes and threads do not break easily. A selection of sizes 80, 90 and 100 is good to start with. You could also buy some 'denim', 'metallic' and 'quilting' needles. Remember that needles need to be replaced regularly and not just when they break!

Crewel needles These are for hand stitching. Buy a packet with various sizes for sewing thick and thin threads.
Other useful items would include a **seam ripper**, not just for undoing stitches but also for guiding fabric underneath the sewing machine teeth; a **tape measure** and a **thimble**.

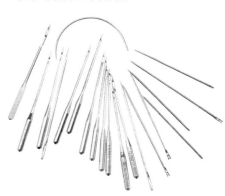

A selection of machine and crewel needles.

Clockwise from top left: a tape measure, fabric scissors, seam ripper, pins, thimble, sharp-pointed scissors and curved scissors.

Embellishments

Beads and sequins come in all shapes and sizes and are a wonderful addition to your purses. Ribbons can be couched down as a background and come in a variety of colours, patterns and widths. Buckles can be sewn on to the purses and brooches can be pinned on with safety pins. Even zips do not have to be boring: you can make them a feature and then look around for charms which can be attached to the ends using split rings. Magnetic clasps can be added for extra security. Shisha glass can be stitched on for shine. I love buttons and you can add them to any of the purses or even completely cover a purse with them. Bondable fibres are fibres that bond together when heated to make a shiny fabric. You can create some wonderful effects with these fibres, as shown on pages 24–25.

Above: beads and sequins.
Left, clockwise from top right: bondable fibres, shisha glass, charms, buckles, magnetic clasps, buttons, zips and ribbons.

Other items

Heavyweight interfacing This is used to give form to some of the purses.

Wadding/batting Natural cotton wadding works well and is nice and flat.

Fusible webbing This is used to bond two fabrics together.

Iron Used to press fabrics and to fix fusible webbing and bondable fibres.

Baking parchment This is used to protect your iron and is also used with bondable fibres. Do not use greaseproof paper.

Freezer paper This is a waxy paper that can be cut into shapes, ironed on to fabric as a template and then sewn round.

Ruler I like the ones used in conjunction with rotary cutters as they come in a variety of lengths and widths, have grid marks printed on them and are see-through. Any ruler would do though.

Craft knife Used for making slits in fabric in order to fit magnetic clasps.

Paper scissors For general cutting.

Round-nosed pliers For fitting magnetic clasps.

Fabric glue sticks, fabric adhesive spray, PVA glue and **spatula** All useful for keeping fabric in place.

Pencil, eraser and sticky tape Useful for making templates and for designing.

Shirring elastic This is used to make fastenings.

Clockwise from top right: an iron, shirring elastic, round-nosed pliers, fabric glue stick, spatula, eraser, pencil, craft knife, sticky tape, grid-marked ruler, wadding (batting), PVA glue, fabric adhesive spray, heavyweight interfacing, freezer paper, fusible webbing and baking parchment.

Design

People are often worried when the word 'design' is mentioned. There is no need. Designing does not have to be complicated. Just concentrating on one or two shapes and then repeating them can be very effective.

Most importantly, choose a subject that you are interested in. You can research your subject by going to your local library or looking it up on the internet. Gather as much information as possible and buy a scrapbook or sketchbook. Every time you find information, photographs or pictures, record this in your book.

I am particularly interested in seed heads – cowslip, hogweed or poppy – and I like to interpret them in machine embroidery. I go out for walks in the country and come back with all sorts of seed heads which I dry and then put them in my sketchbook for future reference. You can see how this led to the free machined design on the Clutch Purse shown on page 51.

For one of the projects in this book, I decided to make an Indian purse (see pages 30–35). The design was partly inspired by Indian bags and fabrics I found in local shops. Prompted by these and other influences, I set to work creating my own Indian designs in my scrapbook.

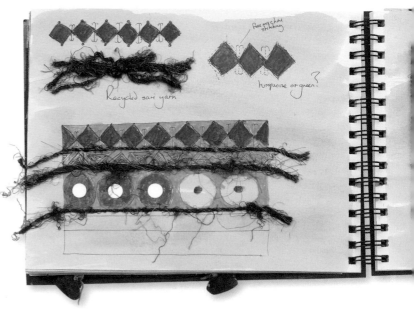

How to start

Getting started on a new project is very exciting. Having decided to start on a project from my Indian scrapbook I went through my fabrics to decide which ones to use. I thought silks and lamés were perfect for this purse and the colour palette I wanted to use was bright jewel colours so I picked out the warm and rich colours shown here.

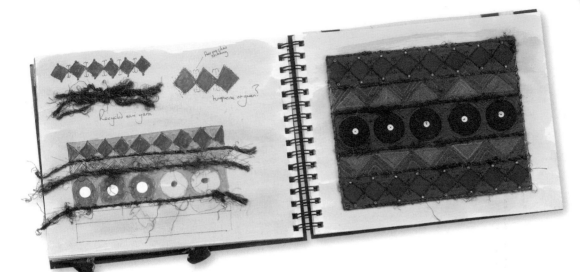

I did the same with my threads, using rayons and metallics. I tend to keep my threads in baskets, sorted into warm, cool or neutral colours. For this project I chose only from the warm and cool selections.

I also picked out embellishments such as velvet ribbons, sequins, beads, sari yarn, shells and shisha glass. You might not end up using all the embellishments you pick out at the beginning of a project, but it is good to have a choice.

This is the fabric I made for the Indian Purse (see pages 30–37). It is decorated with free machine embroidery, beads and sequins, and edged with sari yarn.

17

Techniques
Free machining

This technique will open up a new world of possibilities for your embroidery. It is a very different way of sewing as you are in control of the stitching. You can go in any direction, not just forwards and backwards. You will need to look at your sewing machine manual to see whether you can lower the feed dogs, or if not, cover them with a plate.

Before you start, replace your machine needle with a new one, preferably a size 90 top stitch needle. If you find that your bobbin thread comes through on the top of the fabric you might need to loosen the top tension on your machine.

1. Draw a grid on one of the pieces of fabric using a ruler and a sharp pencil.

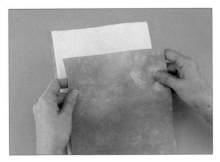

2. Spray the piece of wadding with fabric adhesive spray and lay your marked piece of fabric on top – right side up.

3. Turn the wadding over and spray the other side, then place the remaining piece of fabric on top.

4. Attach the standard foot to your sewing machine and thread the machine with machine embroidery thread. Sew along all the lines to form the grid.

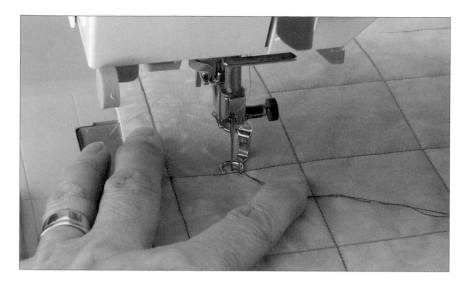

5. Lower the feed dogs and attach the darning foot. Decide which pattern you want to start with – see page 21. Lower the machine needle into the fabric and then raise the needle. This will bring the bobbin thread up to the surface. Holding the two threads to one side, sew one or two small stitches on top of each other to secure.

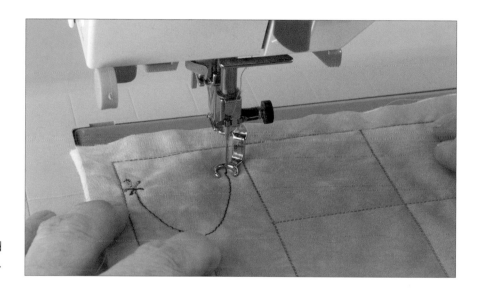

6. Start moving the fabric around to create different shapes.

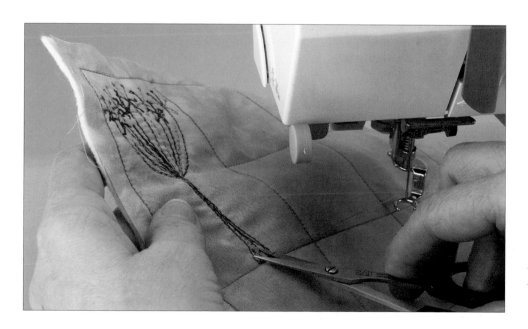

7. When you have finished, snip off the threads with the sharp-pointed scissors.

Free machining patterns

You can either follow my patterns or make up your own. The patterns shown in the sampler opposite were all sewn using free machine methods, which are described in the diagram below.

1 This was inspired by the seed head sketches in my sketchbook.	**2** This design looks like an ammonite fossil. It is best to draw detailed designs on to the fabric before free machining.	**3** These stones can be pebbles or boulders depending on their size and the filling around them, which is a small meandering stitch.
	4 Start in the middle of the design and work your way out. Take the stitch out to each corner and to the top, bottom and each side, then fill in the rest.	**5** Draw the two squares on to the background fabric then fill them in with meandering stitch. Fill in the rest of the block with straight stitch.
6 Draw the chevron pattern on to the background fabric and then fill in with straight stitch.	**7** Lightly draw on the grid pattern and cover with free machining using a narrow zigzag stitch.	**10** Go up and down this block in straight stitch taking the stitch out and in to create the shapes.
8 Draw in the middle square and then fill this in with straight stitch. Move the stitching out a little and sew another five or six rows.	**9** Use a combination of embroidery stitches on your machine to fill in this block.	

Making your own fabric

Making background fabric

One of the simplest ways of making a new background is to cut strips of fabric and weave them together. Different effects can be achieved by using only two fabrics and cutting the strips to the same size, or using lots of different fabrics and cutting the strips to different widths. The sample demonstrated here can be made into a much larger piece if you cut a bigger piece of heavyweight interfacing and longer strips.

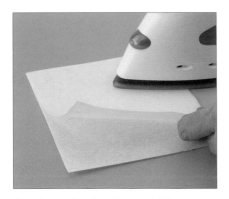

1. Place the fusible webbing on to the heavyweight interfacing and press it with the iron. When this has cooled down, peel off the backing paper.

2. Cut the two pieces of fabric into 2.5cm (1in) strips and lay them on the interfacing, starting at the top left-hand corner. Secure the strips with pins.

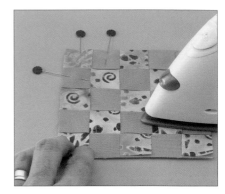

3. When all the strips are in place, press the piece with the iron.

4. Lower the feed dogs on your machine, thread it with the variegated thread and free machine round all the squares, going round each square two or three times.

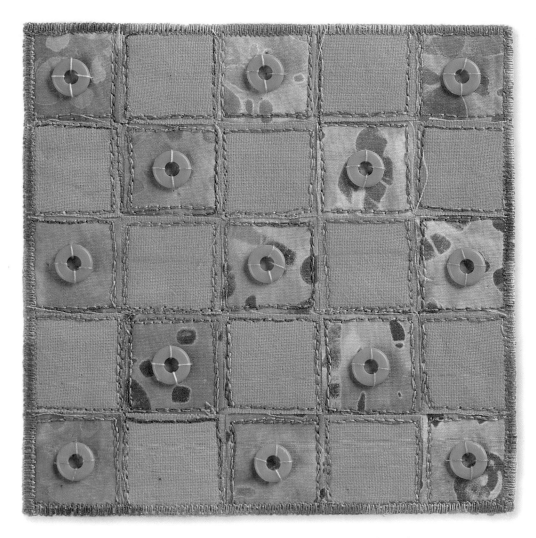

The finished fabric. I have added washer-shaped beads.

This piece uses more than two fabrics and different width strips. Instead of free machining, a machine embroidery stitch has been used.

This piece has been decorated with rows of stitches very close together.

Using bondable fibres

Bondable fibres can add a bit of sparkle to your work. There are two types – Hot Fix and Standard. The Hot Fix fibres bond to themselves when placed between baking parchment and pressed with an iron on a silk setting. This makes a sheet of web-like, non-woven fabric. The Standard fibres will not bond to themselves, but a layer can be put between two layers of Hot Fix.

You will need

Selection of Hot Fix bondable fibres
Baking parchment
Iron

1. Take a piece of baking parchment and sprinkle on a selection of fibres.

2. Place another sheet of parchment on top. Set the iron to the silk setting. Press. Irons vary in temperature, so if the fibres are not bonding, it may be necessary to increase the temperature slightly.

3. When it has cooled down, remove the fabric.

Note

Changing the iron temperature produces different effects (see below). Always try a test piece first to see what sort of effect you want to achieve.

Fibres pressed with a hot iron – they change to matt.

Fibres pressed with a medium iron – they change colour.

Fibres pressed with a cool iron – they remain sparkly.

Bondable fibres can be used in so many ways but I particularly like using two layers and trapping bits in between.

With snipped ribbons.   With snipped threads.   With small sequins.

Here, two sheets of bondable fibres have been made in different colours, cut into strips and woven together, then pressed again.

Pieces of multicoloured thread have been trapped in between two lots of fibres. Lengths of the thread have then been couched down using an invisible thread.

A sheet of bonded fibres has been cut into petal shapes, sewn round and made up into a flower that could be used to embellish a purse.

Fibres have been bonded on to felt and free machined with a spiral.

Using ribbons

Making a background fabric out of ribbons is great fun, and there are such a variety of ribbons in the shops that finding just the colours you need is no problem. Not only haberdashery shops but also florists keep a good supply of ribbons.

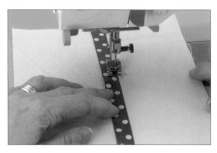

1. Cut a selection of ribbons into 23cm (9in) lengths and, starting in the middle, pin the first ribbon to the background fabric. Sew down each side using invisible thread.

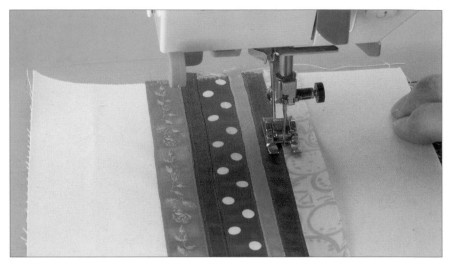

2. Take the next ribbon and pin it down next to the first one. Sew down each side. Continue adding ribbons in this way.

The finished piece.

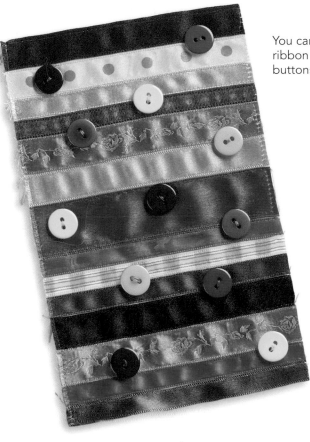

You can embellish
ribbon fabric with
buttons...

...or beads.

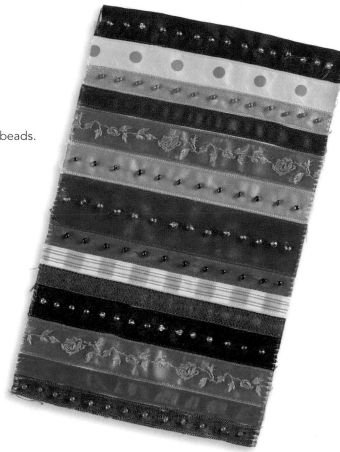

You can add more
ribbons at right angles
to the first ones...

...or add automatic stitches
from your sewing machine
in different threads.

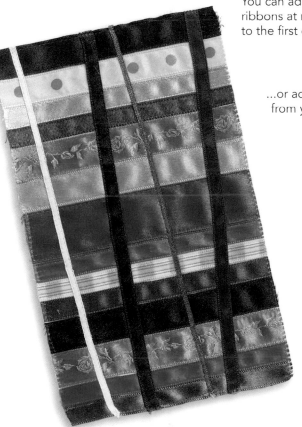

Making embellishments

There are various techniques you can use to embellish your purses and here are some ideas.

Quick brooches

1. Cut out a fabric circle 9cm (3½in) in diameter and with matching thread, make small running stitches close to the edge.

2. Pull the thread tight and make a few stitches to finish off.

3. Sew on a button at the centre of the gathered side.

4. Sew a safety pin on the back.

The finished brooch with some other styles.

Covering a washer with thread

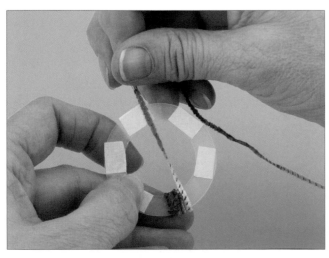

1. Put small pieces of double-sided tape on one side of the washer and peel off the backing. Choose an interesting thread and wind it over the washer until it is covered.

Washers covered in different threads.

Covering a press stud

This technique only works if you use a fine fabric such as silk or lamé.

 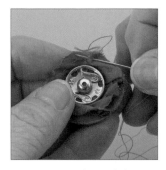  

1. Take a large 15mm (5/8in) press stud and cut two circles of silk 35mm (1³/8in) in diameter. Place the two circles of silk together and position in between the two sides of the press stud. Press together.

2. Using a thread that matches the silk, sew a running stitch around one of the pieces of silk.

3. Pull the thread to gather the silk circle. Make one or two stitches to secure it.

4. Repeat on the other side of the press stud and put in two stitches to finish off.

The covered press stud. When slip stitching the two halves of the press stud on to a background, sew them on loosely or they will keep popping open.

Making a ribbon bow

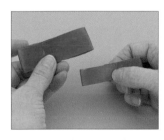 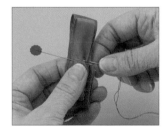 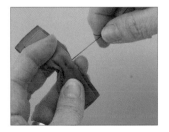 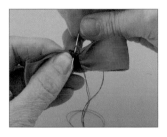

1. Take a length of wide ribbon and fold it as shown, overlapping the ends. Do the same to a shorter length of narrower ribbon.

2. Place the narrower ribbon on top. Measure the middle and put in a pin. Thread a needle and make a few running stitches across the middle of the ribbons.

3. Remove the pin and pull the thread to gather the ribbons.

4. Take a short length of narrow ribbon. Bind it round the middle of the bow and finish off with a few stitches.

The finished ribbon bow with alternative colours.

Indian Purse

Please read all the instructions before starting any of the projects. Note that a 6mm (¼in) seam is used throughout unless otherwise stated.

This purse is inspired by all the beautiful colours found in Indian textiles, colours that you would perhaps not normally put together but which work well in an 'over the top' sort of way!

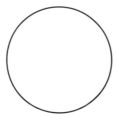

The template for the circle design.

You will need

Sewing machine with darning foot, appliqué foot and zipper foot

Top fabric, 20.3 x 24cm (8 x 9½in)

Wadding, 21.5 x 25.5cm (8½ x 10in)

Thin cotton, 21.5 x 25.5cm (8½ x 10in)

Lining fabric, 20.3 x 24cm (8 x 9½in)

Fabric marking pencil

Pencil and ruler

Fabric scissors

Iron

Fusible webbing, 25.5 x 17.8cm (10 x 7in)

Fabric in three contrasting colours, 15.2 x 10cm (6 x 4in) each

Metallic and rayon threads

Fabric for the inside pockets, 20.3 x 43.8cm (8 x 17¼in)

Fabric adhesive spray

Recycled sari yarn

Invisible thread

Two zips, 17.8cm (7in) each

Press studs

Beads and sequins

Pins

Two cowrie shells

Two split rings

1. Take the top fabric and with the marking pencil draw lines down the length of the fabric measuring from the left-hand side as follows: 5cm (2in); 3.2cm (1¼in); 3.8cm (1½in); 3.2cm (1¼in) and 5cm (2in).

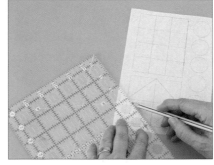

2. Take the fusible webbing and trace six circles from the template, then draw twelve 2.5cm (1in) squares. Draw four 3.8cm (1½in) squares with a diagonal line across each.

3. Cut the fusible webbing into the separate sections as shown and place on top of each of the contrasting fabrics. Press with the iron.

4. Cut out each shape, peel off the paper backing and place the shapes on the top fabric as shown. When you are satisfied that they are in the correct positions, press with the iron.

5. Place the top fabric on top of the wadding and place the thin cotton underneath. Spray the layers with fabric adhesive to keep them in place.

6. Set up your machine for free machining by lowering the feed dogs and putting on a darning foot. Choose a thread that matches the circles in the middle and start by sewing round and round each circle in a spiral shape.

7. Continue sewing round each shape, changing threads where necessary. Finish off by couching down the recycled sari yarn. Use invisible thread to do this and change the stitch to a zigzag.

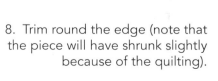

8. Trim round the edge (note that the piece will have shrunk slightly because of the quilting).

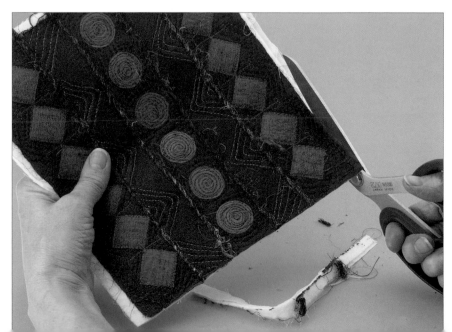

9. Embellish the outside of the purse with beads and sequins.

10. Place the decorated purse fabric on top of the lining fabric and pin all the way round.

11. Put your machine back to normal sewing. Attach the appliqué foot on and sew all round the edge. Trim if necessary.

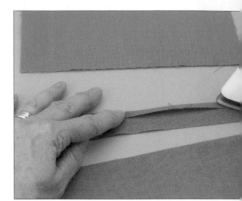

12. Take the fabric for the pockets and cut it into two 20.3cm (8in) squares. The remaining piece will measure 3.2 x 20.3cm (1¼ x 8in). Fold the larger pieces in half and press them. Take the thin strip, turn in 6mm (¼in) each side and press.

13. Place the zips in between the pockets, with the thin strip between the zips as shown. The zips should open from opposite ends. Pin them in place.

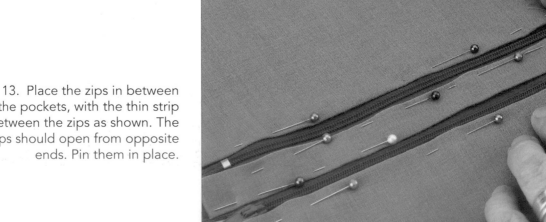

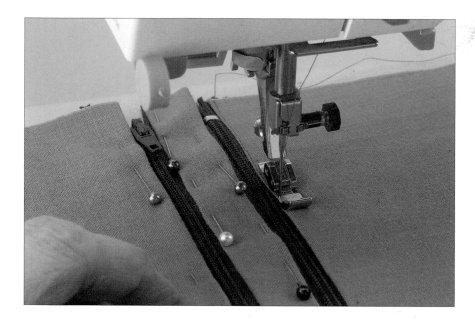

14. Change to the zipper foot and sew in the zips.

15. Place the pockets on top of the main section, wrong sides together, and pin.

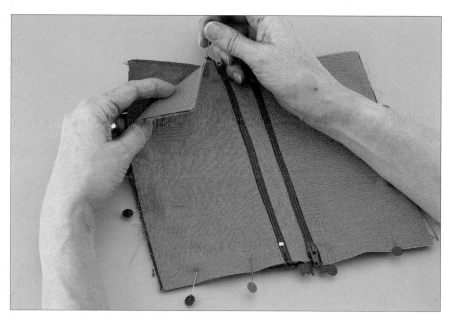

16. Change back to the appliqué foot and with invisible thread top and bottom, sew all around the edge. Trim if necessary.

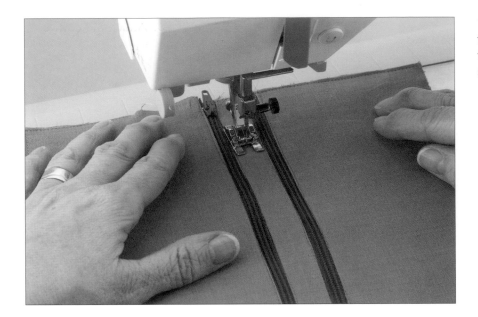

17. Still with the invisible thread top and bottom, sew down the middle of the two zips to separate the pockets.

18. To cover the raw edges, take the sari yarn and place it along the inside edge of the purse. Couch it down with invisible thread using a zigzag stitch. Repeat on the front of the purse.

19. Cover the press studs with one of the contrasting fabrics (see page 29) and attach them to the corners of the pockets.

20. Attach the cowrie shells to the split rings and then to the purse zips.

The finished Indian Purse.

This alternative Indian style purse is decorated with appliqué shapes and sequins and has fabric beads in the corners.

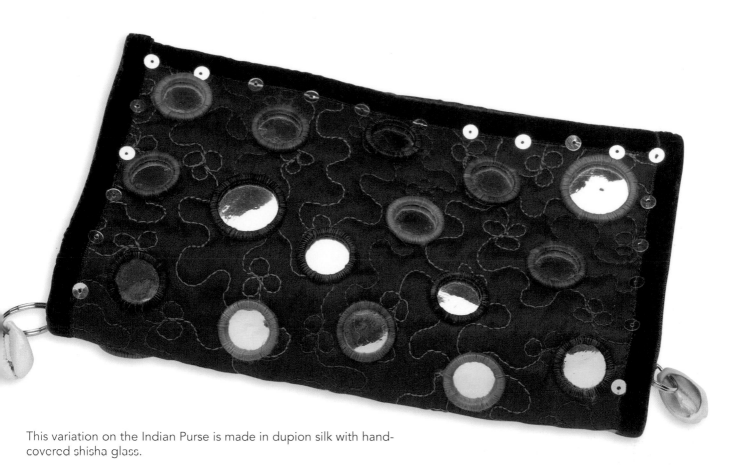

This variation on the Indian Purse is made in dupion silk with hand-covered shisha glass.

This purse was made from part of a cushion cover and has tiny bells added to the split rings.

Frilly Purse

I like to make different textures with my fabrics and lots of pleats make this purse very tactile. You do not need to measure the distance between the pleats: they will look better if they are placed randomly.

You will need

Sewing machine with walking foot, darning foot and zipper foot

Iron

Main fabric, 23 x 45.7cm (9 x 18in)

Wadding, 24 x 30.5cm (9½ x 12in)

Lining, 21.5 x 28cm (8½ x 11in)

Zip, 17.8cm (7in)

Machine thread to match top fabric, zip and lining

Fabric scissors

Pins

Large sequins

Invisible thread

Fabric adhesive spray

1. Take the main fabric, fold it in half and press it. Set your machine for normal sewing and sew 6mm (¼in) from the fold, using the same thread on the top and in the bobbin.

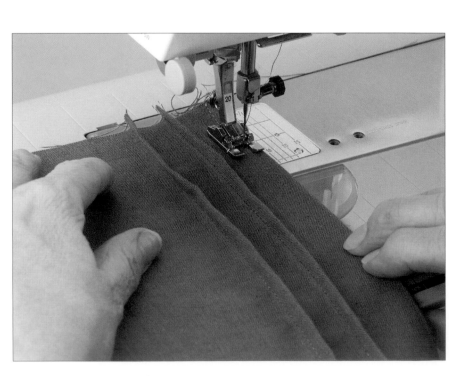

2. Make another fold beside the first one and sew as before. Continue to make a row of pleats from the centre (the first fold) to the edge.

3. Now fold, press and sew pleats from the centre to the other edge. These pleats should face in the opposite direction to the first ones. Make six pleats either side of the centre fold, stopping 2.5cm (1in) from the edges. The finished piece will measure 29cm (11½in).

4. Spray the wadding with fabric adhesive and then place the outer fabric on top.

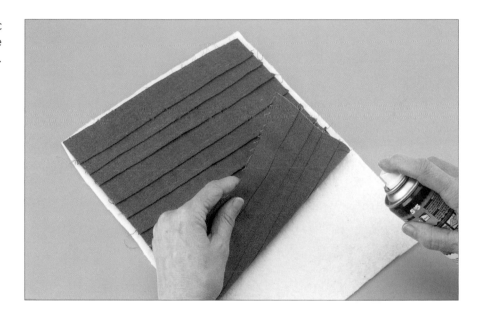

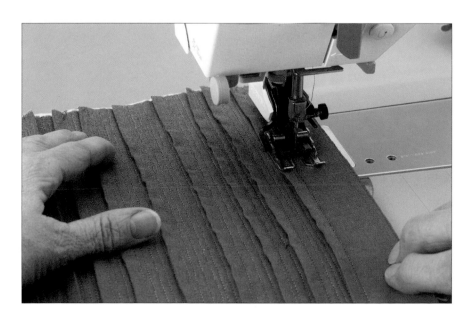

5. Attach the walking foot and using the same thread, sew rows of stitching up and down between the folds. When the sewing is complete, trim the piece down to 21.5 x 28cm (8½ x 11in).

6. Now attach the darning foot and lower the feed dogs. Put invisible thread on the top and in the bobbin. To attach the sequins, start at the edge and sew in approximately 2.5cm (1in). With the needle up, place a sequin on the fabric.

7. Hand turn the wheel so that the needle goes down in to the centre of the sequin.

8. Turn the wheel again so that the needle goes in on the far side of the sequin. Continue sewing to the next sequin position, and cover the outer fabric in this way.

Note

Do not sew sequins too close to the edges as you have to leave room for seam allowances.

9. Take the zip and place it right sides together at the top of the purse. Pin and then tack both edges of the zip.

10. Put the machine back to normal sewing and attach the zipper foot. Using thread to match the zip on the top and in the bobbin, sew down the zip. Open the zip slightly so that you will be able to turn the purse right sides out later.

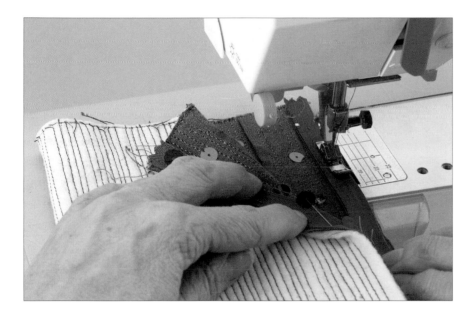

11. Change back to the standard sewing foot and with thread to match the purse, sew down each side. Turn the purse right sides out.

12. Take your piece of lining and fold it in half, right sides together. Sew down each side with a 1.3cm (½in) seam allowance.

13. Turn back the top edges 1.3cm (½in) and press.

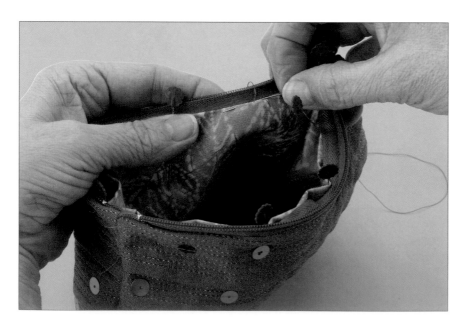

14. Pin the lining inside the purse and slip stitch it in place.

The finished Frilly Purse.

The larger, turquoise frilly purse is decorated with tiny mother-of-pearl beads and a heart charm attached to the zip. The smaller purse is made with purple dupion silk with chunky round beads added and a shoe charm on the zip.

This frilly purse in lime green is decorated with tiny turquoise beads to match the zip, and is finished with a shoe charm.

Clutch Purse

Keeping it simple is sometimes the best policy and this is a simple, classic clutch purse with free machine embroidered seed heads and beads for decoration.

You will need

Sewing machine with walking foot, darning foot and appliqué foot

Top fabric, 23 x 33cm (9 x 13in)

Wadding, 23 x 33cm (9 x 13in)

Lining, 23 x 33cm (9 x 13in)

Narrow ribbon, 99cm (39in) long, cut into three 33cm (13in) pieces

Thread to match top fabric and lining

Invisible thread

Contrasting machine quilting thread

Pins

Small beads

Set of magnetic clasps

Two pieces of heavyweight interfacing, 2.5 x 3.8cm (1 x 1½in)

Round-nosed pliers

Sharp pencil, craft knife and ruler

Fabric scissors

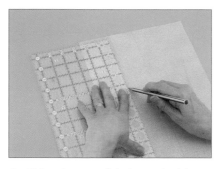

1. Take the top fabric and with a ruler and sharp pencil, lightly draw a line down the middle of the fabric. Draw two more lines, 6.3cm (2½in) either side of this.

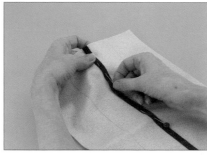

2. Place the fabric on top of the wadding and position one piece of ribbon on the middle line. Pin it down.

3. Attach the walking foot and with invisible thread top and bottom, sew down either side of the ribbon with a straight stitch. Repeat with the other two pieces of ribbon placed on the outer lines.

4. Change to the darning foot, lower the feed dogs and thread your machine with matching machine quilting thread. Sew up and down between the ribbons in wavy lines until the whole surface is covered.

5. Place the purse right side down and fold back 11.4cm (4½in). Pin along the fold. This will be the bottom of the purse.

Note

At this stage, measure the finished piece (it will have shrunk slightly after quilting) and if necessary cut the lining piece of fabric down to size. Put this to one side.

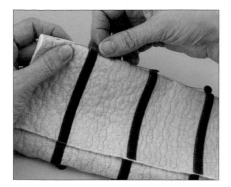

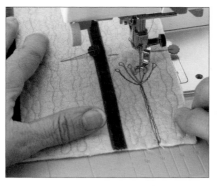

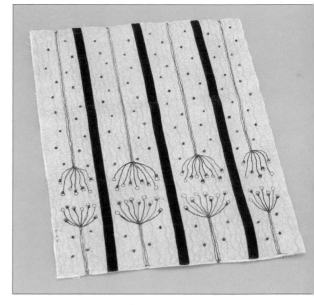

6. Fold down the flap of the purse and pin along the top fold.

7. Change to a contrasting machine quilting thread and start to free machine the seed heads. Start at the bottom of the piece, which will be the purse's flap. Take the seed heads up to the row of pins you made in step 6. This will be the top of the purse.

8. When you have finished the flap, embroider the seed heads on the rest of the purse and sew on the beads as shown.

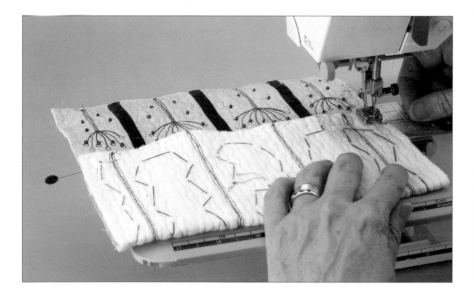

9. Change to the appliqué foot and change the thread to match the top fabric. Fold the main section of the purse, right sides together and sew the outside seams, with a 1.3cm (½in) seam allowance, leaving 1.3cm (½in) at the top for turning.

10. Change your thread to match the lining fabric and sew the outside seams of the lining in the same way, leaving 1.3cm (½in) at the top for turning.

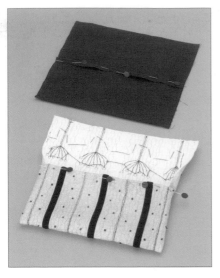

12. Place the purse with the pocket down and then place the lining, also pocket down, on top.

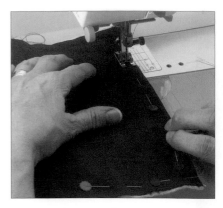

13. Pin then machine sew round the flap.

11. Turn the main section right sides out, but leave the lining as it is. Pin down the 1.3cm (½in) seam allowance on the main section and the lining.

14. Trim off the corners of the flap.

15. To stabilise the magnetic clasp, take one of the pieces of heavyweight interfacing and place it centrally on the top of the purse, just outside the sewn line. Machine sew it down.

Note

When choosing a lining, make sure it is not too thin, as you do not want the heavyweight interfacing to show through.

16. Turn the purse right sides out. Using a sharp craft knife, make two little cuts through both the lining and the heavyweight interfacing and insert the leg part of the magnetic clasp.

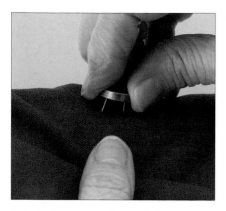

17. Fold up the flap of the purse and insert the clasp as shown.

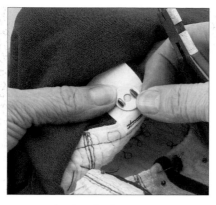

18. Fit the back closure over the legs of the clasp.

19. Fold back the legs of the clasp to secure it, using the round-nosed pliers.

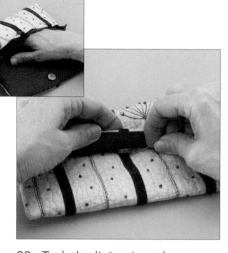

20. Tuck the lining into the purse and fold over the flap. Mark with a pin where the other part of the clasp should be.

21. Hold the other piece of heavyweight interfacing behind the place you have marked with a pin.

22. Make two little cuts through the front of the purse and the heavyweight interfacing, using the craft knife.

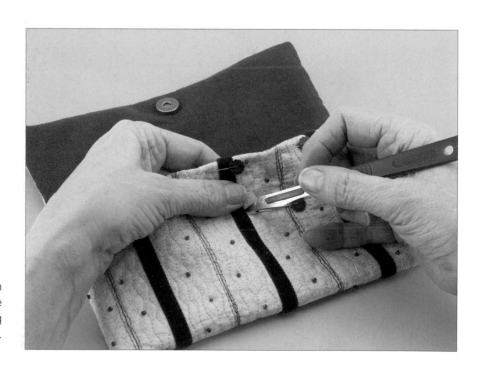

23. Insert the legs of the clasp through the holes as before.

24. Place the back closure over the legs of the clasp and once again turn back the legs using the round-nosed pliers.

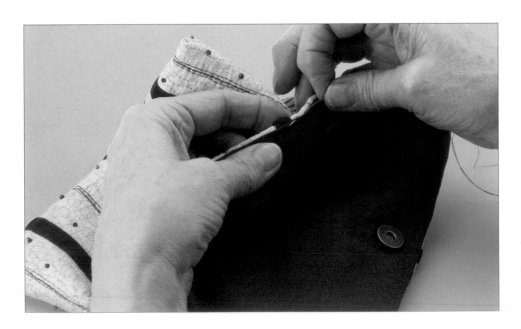

25. Finish off by pinning the lining to the front of the purse and slip stitching it in place by hand.

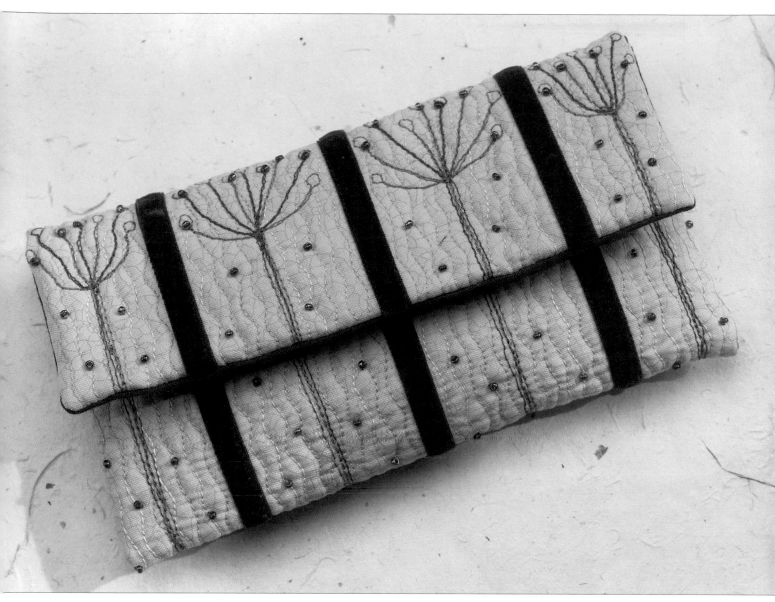

The finished Clutch Purse.

This clutch purse has a strap and buckle and is decorated with hand-embroidered
French knots and straight stitch.

Another clutch purse, made with ribbons as shown on pages 26–27,
with a ribbon bow (see page 29).

This clutch purse has fabric ribbon couched down. The three large washers are covered with the same fabric ribbon.

Daisy Purse

One of my favourite flowers is the daisy as it cheers me up and makes me think of spring time. These little daisies are made by free machining on to heavyweight interfacing, which is an excellent way of creating your own embellishments for purses.

The template for the daisies.

The template for the purse.

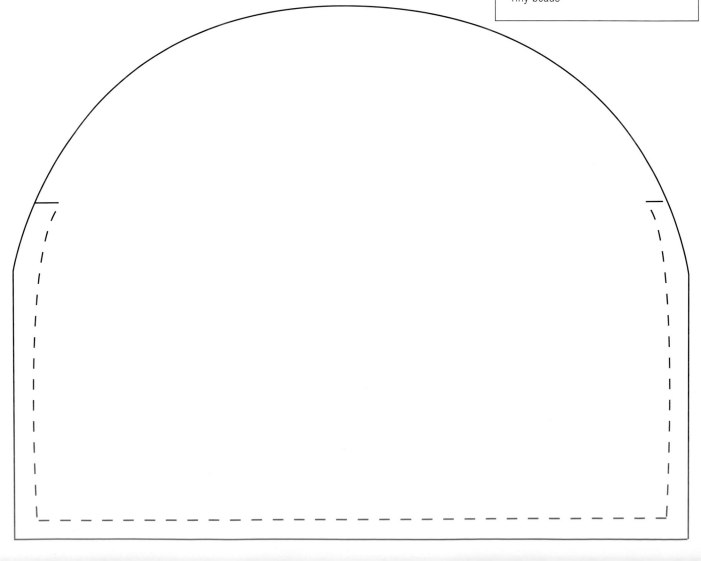

1. Cut the top fabric, wadding and lining into 17.8 x 20.3cm (7 x 8in) pieces. Put the lining pieces to one side. Take one piece of wadding and spray with the fabric adhesive spray, and place one piece of the fabric on top. Do the same with the other pieces of fabric and wadding.

2. Thread the machine with machine quilting thread, lower the feed dogs and attach the darning foot. Free machine all over both pieces of fabric and wadding with a random swirling design.

3. Put the piece of freezer paper over the template, trace it and cut it out. Place it on one of the pieces of quilted fabric, shiny side down and iron it on.

Note

You can reuse freezer paper a number of times.

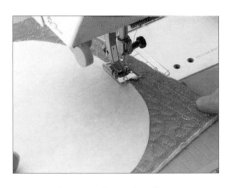

4. Put the machine back to normal sewing and attach the standard foot. Sew all round the outside of the freezer paper. Repeat with the remaining piece of quilted fabric.

5. Cut out the two pieces just outside the sewn line.

6. Place the two pieces right sides together and sew along the lines marked on the template.

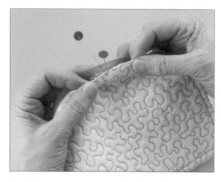

7. Measure the middle of the zip and the middle of the fabric and pin them right sides together.

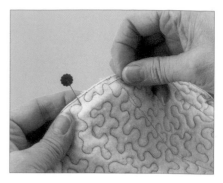

8. Tack in the zip.

9. Change to a zipper foot and sew in the zip.

Note

Undo the zip slightly so that the purse can be turned right sides out later.

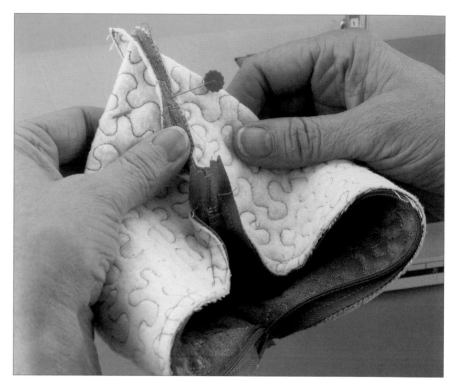

10. Fold the purse to make a triangle of one of the bottom corners as shown. Pin the purse where it measures 5cm (2in) across.

11. Change the machine back to normal sewing. Stitch across the 5cm (2in) base of the triangle. Repeat steps 10 and 11 for the other bottom corner of the purse.

12. Cut off the corner edge pieces just beyond the stitching.

13. Turn the bag right sides out.

14. Transfer the daisy template six times on to the heavyweight interfacing. Press lightly with a sharp pencil.

15. Thread the sewing machine with white thread on the top and in the bobbin. Lower the feed dogs and attach the darning foot. Start sewing the first daisy by stitching round each petal.

16. Fill in the petal with straight stitch. Repeat with all the daisies.

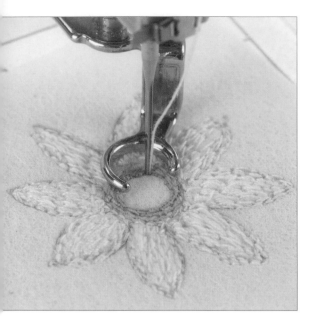

17. Change to yellow thread and fill in the middle of the daisies. Stitch round and round in circles.

18. Cut out the daisies close to the edge of the stitching. Change back to white thread and using a narrow zigzag stitch, go round all the edges of the petals to finish them off.

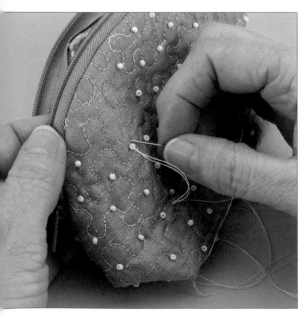

19. Sew the tiny beads on to the background on the purse.

20. Pin the daisies on to the purse and stitch them on by hand with yellow thread, leaving the petals free.

21. Take the two pieces of lining fabric and sew them together in the same way as the outside of the purse. Sew across the bottom corners and cut off the excess as for the purse.

22. Turn over the top of the lining and press it.

23. Pin the lining inside the purse and slip stitch it in place.

The finished Daisy Purse.

This version of the Daisy Purse has machine-embroidered flowers with bead centres, and is finished with a heart charm.

The purse in front has daisy-shaped buttons sewn on; the one behind has
large star sequins with beads at the centres.

Box Purse

This is a very useful, chunky little purse which is covered in buttons for decoration.

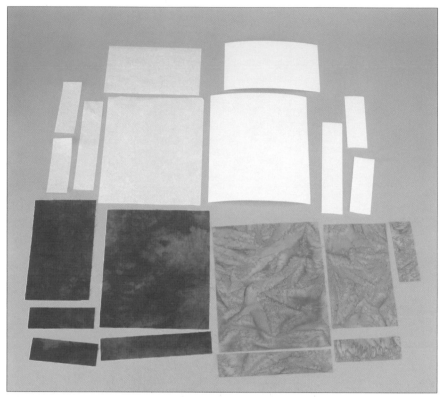

1. Take the top fabric, lining fabric, heavyweight interfacing and fusible webbing and out of each of these cut: one piece, 16 x 19cm (6¼ x 7½in); one piece, 16 x 9.5cm (6¼ x 3¾in); one piece, 16 x 3.2cm (6¼ x 1¼in); and two pieces, 9.5 x 3.2cm (3¾ x 1¼in).

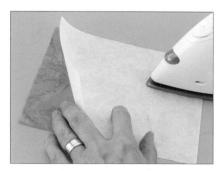

2. Press the fusible webbing on to the back of the top fabric. Let it cool down and then peel off the backing.

3. Press the top fabric with the fusible webbing attached on to the heavyweight interfacing. Do this to all the pieces. Keep the lining fabric to one side for later.

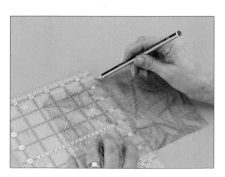

4. Using a sharp pencil, draw lines 3.2cm (1¼in) apart on all the pieces, to make a grid.

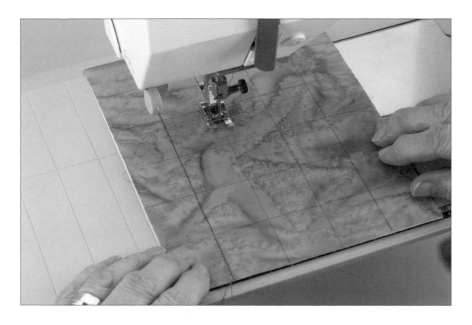

5. Set up your machine with an appliqué foot and contrasting thread. Sew along all the lines, including the edges, with a straight stitch.

6. Using doubled thread that matches the buttons, start sewing them on to the purse. On the smaller main piece, the button on the bottom middle square will be used to fasten the purse. When you sew this button on, wrap the thread round two or three times under the button so that it stands out slightly. If you do not do this, the button will be too tightly attached and the clasp might pull it off.

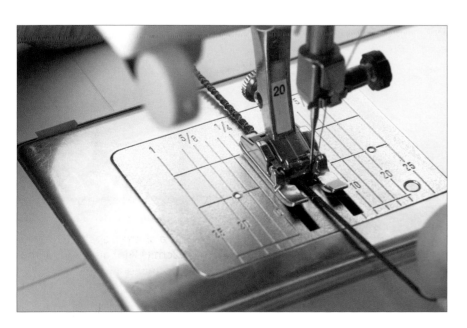

7. To cover the shirring elastic, use an appliqué foot. Set the stitch to a narrow zigzag and use a thread that matches the buttons on the top and in the bobbin. Holding the shirring elastic taut and leaving 2.5cm (1in) at either end, start to cover the elastic with the thread.

8. Sew over the shirring elastic two or three times until it is completely covered. Trim it down to 7.6cm (3in).

9. Fold the elastic into a loop and place it on the wrong side at the top of the larger main piece. Place a piece of sticky tape over it to stop it moving. With the same thread, make three or four stitches to keep the elastic in place.

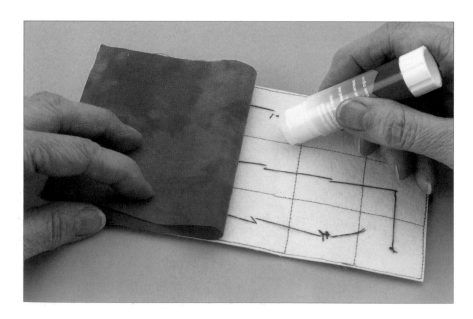

10. Take your lining pieces and the fabric glue stick and starting on the smaller main piece, rub the glue stick over the back of the interfacing and place the lining on top. Do this to all the other pieces.

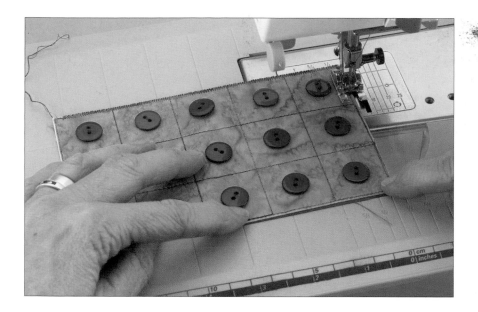

11. Change the stitch to a narrow zigzag and sew all the way round all of the pieces.

12. To sew the purse together, open up the zigzag and widen the stitch. Start by sewing the base to the bottom of the larger main piece.

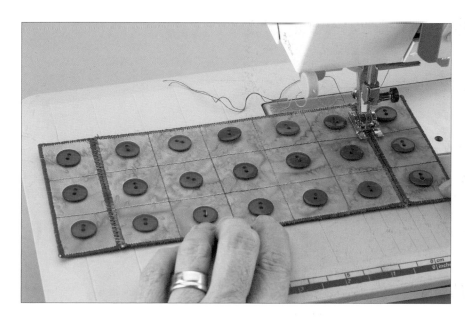

13. Then sew each side to the smaller main piece.

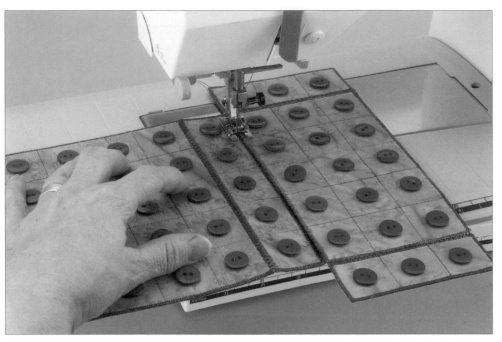

14. Then sew the smaller main piece to the base, making sure that the button used for fastening the purse is in the correct position.

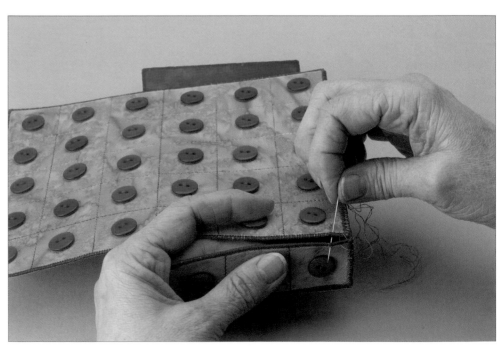

15. Lastly, thread up a needle with the same thread you have been using and sew up the remaining sides, overstitching by hand.

The finished Box Purse.

The tiny box purse in front has machine-embroidered appliqué circles with buttons sewn on;
the one behind it features chunky beads sewn on by hand with embroidered straight stitches.

This vibrant box purse is decorated by buttons in all the colours of the rainbow.

Velvet Purse

I love luxurious fabrics such as velvet and silk and wanted to make a purse out of them that would just sit in my hand. The magnets hidden inside the top pieces make an excellent invisible fastening.

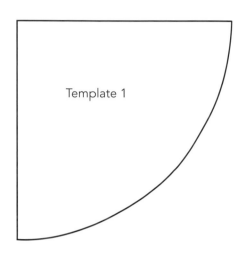

Template 1

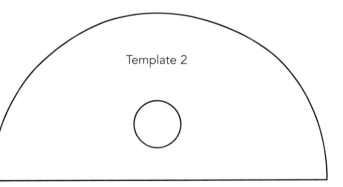

Template 2

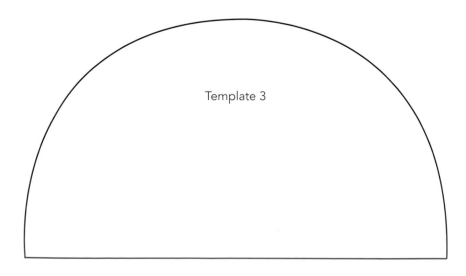

Template 3

You will need

Sewing machine with appliqué foot and darning foot

For the main purse:

Two pieces of velvet, 21.6 x 15.2cm (8½ x 6in)

Two pieces of fusible webbing, 21.6 x 15.2cm (8½ x 6in)

Two pieces of calico, 21.6 x 15.2cm (8½ x 6in)

Two pieces of lining, 21.6 x 15.2cm (8½ x 6in)

Variegated gimp for couching down on the velvet

Invisible thread

Fabric scissors

Iron

Sharp pencil and ruler

Card for templates

Pins

Needle for hand sewing

For the top:

Heavyweight interfacing, 20.3 x 10cm (8 x 4in)

Fusible webbing, 20.3 x 10cm (8 x 4in)

Silk, 28 x 12.7cm (11 x 5in)

Fabric glue stick, PVA glue and spatula

Seed beads

Two magnets

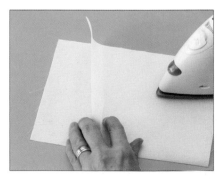

1. Starting with the main purse, take one piece of fusible webbing and press it on to one of the pieces of calico.

2. Peel off the paper backing and press the calico on to one of the pieces of velvet. Repeat with the remaining pieces.

3. Thread your sewing machine with invisible thread and attach a standard foot. Change the stitch to a zigzag. Starting in the middle, couch down the gimp in straight lines down the velvet. Repeat with the other piece of velvet.

4. Place both pieces right sides down, making sure that the nap is going in the same direction. Draw a pencil line down the middle. Then measure 5cm (2in) either side of the original line and draw lines on either side. Repeat for the other piece of velvet.

5. Put right sides together. Transfer the template 1 shape on to card. Place the template on each of the bottom corners and draw round it to make rounded corners.

6. Cut out the rounded corners.

7. Take one of the pieces and fold it on the middle line. Place a pin 1.3cm (½in) in. Fold on the other lines and do the same. Repeat for the other piece.

8. Pin all the way round leaving 3.2cm (1¼in) free at the top either side.

9. Place the two pieces right sides together. When you have two folds facing each other, make sure you push one one way and one the other as shown.

10. Change the thread on your machine to match the velvet and sew all round the purse using a 1cm (³/₈in) seam allowance. Turn the purse right sides out.

11. Take the two pieces of lining and follow steps 4–8. Change the thread to match the lining fabric and sew all round the lining using a 1cm (³/₈in) seam allowance and leaving 3.2cm (1¼in) free at the top either side.

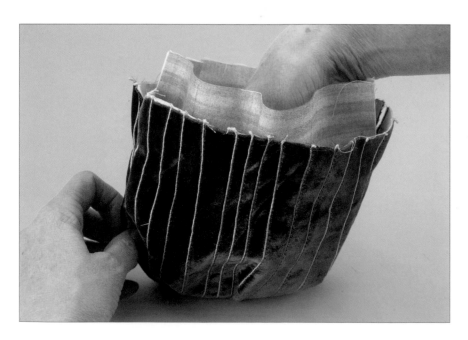

12. Place the lining in the purse.

13. Pin all round the top.

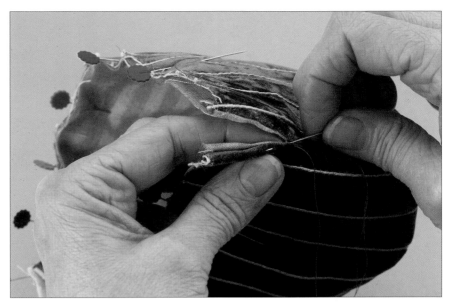

14. Turn in the side seams and slip stitch them down.

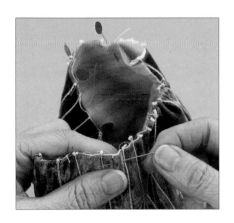

15. Thread a needle with the thread that matches the velvet and using it double, running stitch across the top of each side of the purse.

16. Gather each side of the purse until it measures 7.6cm (3in) across.

17. Transfer template 2 on to card, place it on top of the heavyweight interfacing and draw round it four times. Cut the shapes out. Do the same on the fusible webbing.

18. Transfer template 3 on to card, place it on the silk and draw round it four times with a dark pencil on light fabric or a light pencil on dark fabric. Cut out the silk shapes.

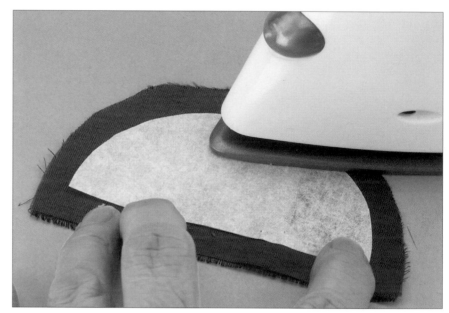

19. Place one piece of fusible webbing on to a piece of the silk and press it with an iron.

20. Peel off the backing and place the silk on top of a piece of the heavyweight interfacing. Press with the silk uppermost, since the heat of the iron cannot penetrate through the heavyweight interfacing.

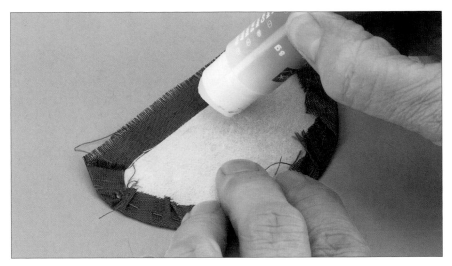

21. Thread a needle with thread that matches the silk and then gather round the edge and pull the thread tight. Sew two or three little stitches to finish off.

22. Use a fabric glue stick along the base of the semicircle of heavyweight interfacing.

23. Fold over the silk edge and stick it down. Repeat steps 19–23 to make four semicircular pieces.

24. Lower the feed dogs and attach a darning foot. Using your chosen thread, free machine all over two of the pieces in a swirling pattern.

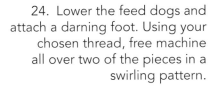

25. Sew beads on to each of these free machined pieces with matching thread, being careful not to go too close to the edge.

26. Take the two remaining pieces. Put a small amount of PVA glue on the back of each magnet and place one on the back of each piece, referring to template 2. Leave until dry.

27. Change your machine back to normal sewing with an appliqué foot and place invisible thread on the top and in the bobbin. Take one of each of the top pieces. Place wrong sides together and sew all round the semicircle, really close to the edge. Do the same with the other two pieces.

28. Place one of the tops over one side of the gathered main purse, pin it in place and sew along the edge. Do the same to the other side.

The finished Velvet Purse.

This sumptuous velvet purse has tiny buttons sewn on and is finished with a handmade brooch (see page 28).

This purse was made with hand-dyed velvet. The pattern on the top was machine embroidered.

The threads couched down on this velvet purse were hand-dyed. The top is made from dupion silk.

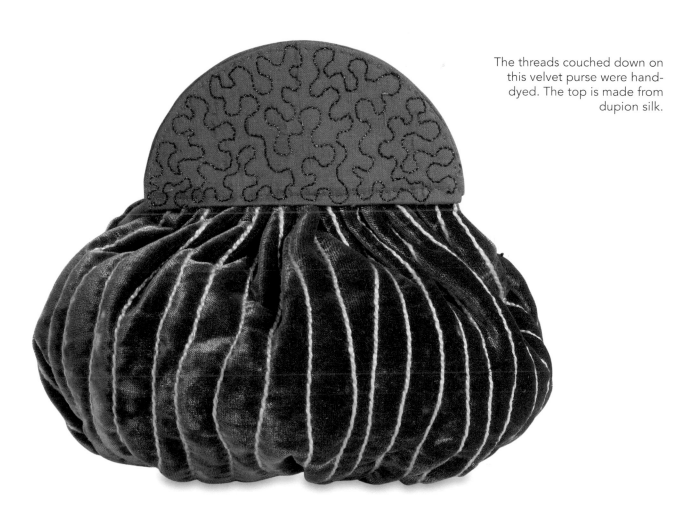

Index